Living with Joy

Poems of courage and hope

Claire-Louise Price

Matador
Unit E2 Airfield Business Park,
Harrison Road, Market Harborough,
Leicestershire. LE16 7UL
Tel: 0116 2792299
Email: books@troubador.co.uk
Web: www.troubador.co.uk/matador
Twitter: @matadorbooks

ISBN 978 1803132 563

British Library Cataloguing in Publication Data.
A catalogue record for this book is available from the British Library.

Typeset in 11pt Aldine401 BT by Troubador Publishing Ltd, Leicester, UK

Matador is an imprint of Troubador Publishing Ltd

Living
with
Joy

Warmest wishes,

Claire-Louise

May
2023

For my Mother
Mary Elizabeth Price

Contents

Living with Joy

Author's Note

Conversation in Devon

'You ought to write a third' she said,
'Then it would be a trilogy'

'Wait a minute' I replied,
'I've only just published the second!'

What I did not say to my beautiful goddaughter
-how could I?
Not yet, too soon
Was that I had thought of a title already.
If more poems turned up
If a third book ever got written
It would be called *Living with Joy*.

Joy was the name of her Mother.

All author profits from the sale of
this book will be donated to
Cancer Research UK

Foreword

These poems were all written during the global pandemic, but they are not about that. Rather, they capture moments in time that enhanced my life, bringing much needed comfort, joy, and eventually a return of confidence.

Confidence, that intangible quality, had taken more of a battering than I realised. Like a lot of people, I found the initial shock followed by the relentless whirr of the pandemic, drained my energy even when life seemed to be returning to normal. A bit like a mobile phone with too many apps open, my batteries were silently running down. All creative energy dissipated and seemed to have disappeared forever.

In May 2020, after walking in the leafy woods and parks of south London, I wrote 'Song of the Trees', my first poem for more than a year. It is about the comfort of Nature in challenging times. I was beginning to think it would be my last as summer gave way to autumn and no more poems appeared.

But in September 2020 I noticed a weekly poets' workshop was being offered online by Oxford University department of continuing education. It was going to be live, with discussion with other poets and guidance from a tutor.

It might be a bit too academic, I thought, and anyway I cannot write poems to order, they just turn up. Probably not for me. A day later, I signed up anyway, more out of desperation than anticipation of a result.

It worked. Far from feeling constrained by a prescribed theme, I responded positively to our tutor Edward Clarke who would say 'Here are the rules for this poetic form. Now follow them, or break them, as much as you want. And if you don't like the theme for this week, write about something else instead!'

Poems started to appear, at first like a gently babbling stream, and then a flowing river. In the third term, when I wrote the title poem 'Living with Joy', they became a cascading waterfall.

Suddenly, I had 30 poems where before there was only one. Enough to publish my third collection, to form a trilogy with my first two books 'Walking with Angels' and 'Dancing with Love'.

Excited and relieved, I could now ask my friend and talented artist Paola Minekov if I could use images of her wonderful paintings to illustrate this third book. Eight works from Paola's portfolio are featured in my previous two books. Imagine my delight when she offered to paint some original new works to illustrate the poems. Her paintings are like gems, enhancing and adorning the poems with vibrant colour, artistic form and a different creative energy.

Living with Joy

It seemed appropriate to name this book 'Living with Joy' as it describes the continuation of my journey through widowhood, and how I learned to find joy in moments of challenge, of calm, or of unexpected serendipity, moments we can all relate to as we go about our daily lives.

Claire-Louise Price
April 2022

Song of the Trees

Trees communicate?
That sounds wrong
Yet while out walking
I heard their song –

'We know, we know'
Swished the sycamores
'We can sense your fear right now
Seeping through our bark'

'We are listening'
Lilted the limes
'Our leaves, fluttering in the breeze,
Are finely tuned'

'We are with you'
Wept the willows
'Your reflection in the water
Says it all'

'Be still'
Breathed the beeches
'Come and rest awhile
Under our boughs'

'Have courage'
Murmured the mighty oak
'Be calmed by our canopies
Be grounded by our roots
Take comfort from the wisdom of the trees
We hear and we are here.'

Seascape

After weeks confined in London
Longing for the sea
I stood on Aldeburgh beach
Breathing in the salty tang of freedom

And yet – the view was too wide
A vast, wispy Suffolk sky
Blending with the endless sea
A shingle shoreline stretching on and on
For miles in both directions

Unable to take in a scene
Beyond their field of vision
My eyes still ache at the memory
A seascape unframed
Like the words of a poem

        Escaping its form and running off the page

The Bard and The Shard

A bronze statue of the Bard
Sits in the cathedral yard
Penning thoughts. It must be hard
To do that, when his view is marred,
His tranquil setting rudely jarred
By the building of the Shard.

What did our best poet say
When his peace was snatched away?
Could he still write every day?
Did inspiration go astray?
I like to think he stopped to pray
Then write a sonnet anyway.

St Paul de Vence

A painting bathed in Provençal sunlight
A hilltop town, a sky of azure blues
Old terracotta roofs contrasting bright

With ancient walls in cream and golden hues.
Beneath an arch which spans a narrow street
In deep shade stand a trio sharing news

How often, I have wondered, do they meet?
By 'our' hotel, the flower decked Lion d'Or
Is this the place they congregate and greet?

They've welcomed me so many times before –
I've stepped into the painting for respite
From nursing kids with mumps, and other chores

The alley is so angled it invites
The viewer to walk in and join the group
Then savour many Provençal delights

Rich lavender, pink rosé, warm fish soup
Deriving comfort from this magic place
My thoughts go round in longing, in a loop.

Stations

As the train heads North
It stops to collect stations.
Passengers are incidental
To this rhythmical ritual
Announcing, slowing, halting
Waiting, smoothly drawing
Away and speeding on
Until the next scheduled stop.
Peterborough, Grantham, Newark, York
Each town a different coloured bead
Is threaded onto a string of rails.
The pattern is repeated South, East and West
Bedford to Brighton
Nottingham to Norwich
Swindon to Swansea

Are joined together with all stops in between.
To transient passengers
Staring idly through the window
Sipping tea
These places are a sign on a platform
Neatly lettered for visibility
To locals these names are symbols
Of welcome and farewell
A gateway to and from their daily lives
In the town they call Home.
A word we can all understand
So by the end of its journey
The train has crafted
Not a necklace of different beads
But a string of identical pearls.

Ariadne

I know what it's like
To be stranded on Naxos
But there the similarity
With Ariadne
Ends. That summer
The ferries were on strike

No Bacchus for me
Leaping with vigour
From his cheetah-drawn chariot
Replacing a faithless lover
In a heartbeat
Entwining me passionately

Titian's painting gives us a clue
What might happen next
Nubile Ariadne
Hailing a ship
Is startled, she recoils
Half naked, revealing
Voluptuous curves
Draped in red and blue

Bacchus is clad in light red
Befitting a lover of wine
The air between them
Fizzes with tension
He is portrayed
Leaping towards her
Almost naked
A robe billows over his head

A plume of white smoke
Appears in the distance
The ferry draws near
This time, no myth.
Tying my blue and red shawl
On my shoulders
I board the crowded boat
And see its name
Ariadne
So in the end I was rescued
By a woman, not a bloke.

Road to the Beach

Slabs of ridged concrete
Surfaced with loose sand
Flip flopped by tourists
Edged on one side by
Humdrum houses
End of town shops, a launderette
Motorbike repairs, no cars
Locals busy talking,
Sitting on upturned crates.

To the left, further on, a landmark
A decrepit windmill with broken sails
Surveying scrubland and scavenging cats.
Quickening pace, leaving the town
Then slowed by an uphill trudge
In the Mediterranean sun
Overheating, needing water, no shade.

A makeshift bridge of wooden planks
Spans a wide ditch, a hazard
An approaching quadbike doesn't slow
Roars across, exhaust blaring smoke
And gets away.

Finally the road gives up
Morphing into a rutted track
One more trek up a final slope and there it is –
A white sandy tree lined beach
Shelving gently down to meet
Tiny wavelets of a calm blue bay
And not a soul in sight.

The slog along the dusty road
Recedes into the distance
Overtaken by a cool refuel
An energising, refreshing dip
In the sparkling waters
Of the Aegean Sea.

The Cottage

I woke and saw the sunlight lighting up a door
It made a diamond pattern, one I hadn't seen before
My first night in a cottage which nestles by the sea
I'd longed to have a pretty base to write my poetry
It's cosy and inviting, and painted Suffolk pink
I bought it on the spot, didn't care what others think
A cottage bought in minutes? I knew I risked derision
My gut was clearly saying I must take a bold decision.

My husband would have loved it, his wisdom spurred me on
'You really need to forge your own path after I am gone
Have courage, have your moment, it's all we ever get
If it all goes pear shaped you can always buy to let
But if you really love it you can make it your own space
It will be your sanctuary, a healing, happy place.'

Willpower

Have some cheese … Yes please – Had enough plum duff… – No more wine? That's fine Mince pie? Not I – Had enough – Plum duff –

February 2021:
A Space Odyssey

Ping! goes my phone
A text – I groan
'Easyjet our sale ends soon'
Might as well fly to the moon
Fed up now as I can't travel
Life is starting to unravel
In the garden to revive
Spot a flower still alive
Looking at it carefully
In the petals I can see
Tiny orbs of golden light
Specks of pollen shining bright
Right beneath my very nose
A solar system in a rose.

A Sprinkling of Thyme

He chopped and stirred into the pot
Tasted and seasoned and chopped some more
As the winter soup bubbled on the stove
And the shorter day drew in
Three friends sat in comfortable chairs
Talking of milestones by candlelight.
As the winter soup bubbled on the stove
And the aroma wafted through the house
It heard plans for a birthday, an anniversary.
It heard of recent deaths. Of babies being born
One, two, three and more
Each bringing joy to a story
Recounted, reminisced, relived.
These stories were caught up by the aroma
Carried into the kitchen
And tipped into the pot with a sprinkling of thyme
The winter soup bubbled on the stove
Combining the humble ingredients
Into an alchemy of human life.

Making Lemonade

Every single week, on Thursday, when I came home from school
She made lemonade
In a huge mixing bowl
I watched her squeeze the juice and grate the golden zest
Pour steaming hot water and glistening sugar
And stir and stir with a wooden spoon
Creating a swirl as if her life depended on it
Finally tapping against the rim – one, two, three,
While I inhaled the warm, heady scent
And watched yellow lemon slices whirl
Round and round
Until they stilled, like lilies on a pond.
I didn't know
When I was six years old, watching intently,
That every pinch of zest contained a dash of wisdom
Every drop of juice distilled a mother's love
And every ounce of sugar poured in a ton of fortitude
All I knew was this heady, citrus brew
Was reassuringly the same, every single week.

My Last Prime Minister

There goes my last Prime Minister
Ushered from the door
Cowed just like the rest of them
I've seen it all before

Their chests unpuffed, their words rebuffed
Their pride dragged in the mud
Their fellow politicians smirking
Baying for their blood

When they arrived to be sworn in
They confidently strutted
They didn't know that they would go
Well and truly gutted

Their starry eyes betrayed the prize
To kiss my hands their goal
Their rampant egos ran amok
Ambition without soul

Fifteen UK Prime Ministers
Had audiences with me
Every week they got more meek
The change was plain to see

Affairs of state foreseen too late
All thoughts in disarray
They often asked me what to do
And what, or not, to say

In sixty years upon the throne
I've learned a thing or two
Prime Ministers are all the same
Red, blue or any hue

Politicians come and go
Their fortunes rise and fall
But I'm still here to give support
To them and to us all

What time is it? It's half past three
Just time to watch the race
Before I swear the next one in
And meet her face to face.

Between the dawn
and the day

A sleepless night well spent
Wrestling with a decision
Toss and turn, a tussle, yes or no
It could go either way

Between the dawn and the day
While night gently softens its inky cloak
Resisting, then yielding to sunrise
Minds are made up

A message will be sent
Regret will be expressed
Prisoners will be freed
Buttons won't be pressed
Bridges will be built
Hope will stay alive
Borders will reopen
Nations will survive

In the no-man's land
Between the dawn and the day
Time for an hour's slumber
Before lives are changed.

Maelstrom

Autumn leaves whirl and twirl and swirl
Around dropping slowly, slowly to the
Ground. Get out the broom and briskly, briskly
Sweep. Allow the lawn to breathe, inhaling
Deep.

Anxious thoughts whirl and twirl and swirl
Around clogging up my head. Get out the mental
Broom give them a sweep, allow my brain
Room to think, to breathe, inhaling
Deep.

My Mum in hospital, a son, a friend,
A niece, unwell. Worrying won't help, so sweep.
Sweep away the worries that whirl and twirl and swirl
Sweep them away, inhale slow and gradually yield to
Deep
Deep
Peace.

The Spring Theme

Sitting at the old pine table in the kitchen
What can I write about spring?
She wondered
Something different, unusual
Not done before?
I could follow the trail of the Troubadors
Celebrating springtime in France
Or simply write an English Hey nonny no
That kind of thing

Or, she pondered
Spring means renewal
Of life and love
I wrote about that
In my Winter poem
A 'Spring is the end of winter
In more ways than one' theme

Perhaps, she imagined,
Spring could be a play on words
Recalling the powerful burst
Of water up from the depths
Into the mysterious pool
Surrounded by whispering birches
A 'spring is the source of a river' theme

Or maybe, she reflected,
Spring symbolising an
Eternal fountain of creativity
Within. It bubbles up and
Spills out onto the page, or the
Canvas, or the musical score, theme

And then there's Wordsworth's poem
But I'm in London, not the Lakes
She sighed and put down her pen
And looked up, then looked again, amazed.
In the vase in the centre of the table
The unpromising bunch of daffodils in greenish bud
Had silently opened in the warmth to reveal
A bouquet of golden, triumphant, abundant glory.
A celebration of everything
Joyful
And so, the poem was written
About the Spring.

Colour Power

As I woke up sleepily
One morning in September
A blue tit lit upon the sill
A moment I remember

The sash was open, he peered in
A cheeky, bobbing fellow
What message do you bring to me
In your blue and yellow?

I wore my yellow cardigan
A patterned dress in blue
And everywhere I went that day
The sun came shining through

'You've brought the sunshine with you
Though today it's cloudy weather.
What gave you the impetus
To wear those two together?'

And I replied 'A blue tit
Landed on my sill today
He chirpily encouraged me
To brighten up your day!'

The Blackbird

My name's Kevin
And I don't care
What you all think
I'll stand right there

I'll strut around
In my new black
I'll look real cool
I've got the knack

You're uncool parents
Don't you know?
Don't tell me when
And where to go

Your frantic warnings
I'll ignore
I like it here
You're such a bore

'Look out! Look out!'
What do you mean?
There's no feline
To be seen

Ouch! It got me
With its claws
It's not my fault
Cats break the laws

But I escaped
And that's a fact
A few lost feathers
But still intact

Why is it
That grown ups know
Exactly when
And where to go?

I won't admit it
No, not me
I'll pose instead
Upon a tree

But ever since
That fateful dawn
I never strut
Upon a lawn.

Dandelion Deadline

He's getting out the lawnmower
Oh no
My precious seeds await the wind
    To blow
Within the softness of my seeding
        Sphere
I have a magic secret hidden
           Here
My puffball is not everything it
Seems
Attached to it are Queen Titania's
    Dreams
A plea to Oberon, the Fairy
      King
She asked us to transmit, by puffball
        Wing
She called upon the dandelion
Mob
She knows that we can really do the
    Job

Entrusted by her, we did what we
                    Could
Her words are destined for the local
                    Wood
Where Oberon resides in all his
Splendour
Titania's message says 'I do
            Surrender'
This truce will help all fairies to
                Survive
This topsy turvy world and start to
                        Thrive
Her contrite words could not be any
Clearer   .
Oh where's the breeze?
That mower's
Getting
Nearer.

Equations

I can't do maths, I never could
I hated it at school
And never would have understood
Why algebra was cool

Add and subtract and multiply
Now all that did make sense
But I won't lie, x minus y
Made me very tense

Algebraic formulae
Designed to be so hard
Aren't really my cup of tea
I'd rather win at cards

Or play roulette, or bet online
Or fix a cricket score
In real life the x and y
Aren't needed any more

I count the stolen banknotes
Divide up all the loot
Negotiate the going rate
To bribe them not to shoot

Just add, subtract or multiply
Algebra's the pits
Success in life's not x and y
I simply use my wits.

Autumn Fruits

September
Ends
And
Summer's
Over
Now.

October
Fruits

Mature
Into
Softness,
Trees
Surrender

Autumnal
November
Delights.

Memories of
Enjoyment
Linger
Long
Over
Winter

Fecund
Ripe
Unctuous
Intenseley
Tangy
Fruits of
Unsurpassed
Lusciousness
Nurturing
Eternal
Seeds of
Spring

(this acrostic poem forms the first line of Ode to Autumn by John Keats)

Road to Autumn

Sixty years along the road
Got my pension – getting old
No longer anybody's wife
I've reached the autumn of my life
Spring and summer were the best
But how do I enjoy the rest?
Think what autumn means to me –
Leaves all dropping from a tree?
That seems too much like an end,
Cold winter waiting round the bend
Ah – scarlet, yellow, orange, gold
Copper, russet, hues in bold
Triumph over fading green
Vivid richness, yet serene
Trees, woods, fields in autumn glory
Now that paints a different story
Hold that thought – and life's begun
A cornucopia of fun.

Arisen

A fire destroyed
The much loved
Village church
At Christmas 1992
Congregation and community were churchless, out of the blue
And then five years of wrangling and bureaucracy ensued
Do we rebuild in the same style, or something new?
Why is a City architect appointed, and foreign too?
What could he know
Of the long history?
Why he was chosen
Is a mystery.
Defying opposition
To the hilt
The committee aged
Controversy raged
But the church
Got itself rebuilt.
One day it rose again
The sun's rays lit up
A huge spire of glass
So all around were
Dazzled, saying
What is this,
Which has come to pass?

A Bientôt

Tu ne seras pas loin
Est ce que tu comprends?
Tu entends ce que je dis?
Ce pays inconnu où tu vas
Est tout près d'ici.

Quant à nous qui restons
Ce ne sera pas longtemps
Après ton depart
Qu'on se retrouvera.
Dans toute l'éternité
Vingt, trente ans –
Qui sait exactement?
Sont un seul petit instant.
Un éclat – et voila!
Nous sommes à nouveau ensemble.

See you soon

You will not be far. Do you understand? Are you listening to what I am saying? This unknown country where you are going is very close by.

As for we who remain, it will not be long after you go that we meet again. In all eternity, twenty, thirty years – who knows exactly? – are one tiny instant. A flash – and there! We are together again.

The Heart of Winter

Dying embers burn and glow
Dimming with each passing hour
Final flickers turn to ash
Gradually getting cold
Like flames of love
Kindled in spring's happy light
Ablaze in summer's fiery heat
Warmed by autumn's mellow sun
Extinguished by the cold white frost
Of winter.
Days yield to night
Skies fall silent
Birds are still
Trees are bare
And yet, like nature, we use this fallow time
To grieve, to rest, to heal
For winter's stark mantle
Envelopes new life
Winter is not dead, it only sleeps
All the while preparing quietly within
To renew and come to vibrant life.
Know too, for you, that
Spring will come again.

Musically speaking

A poem
Is a symphony
of Timbre
Tonality
Lilt
Cadence
Rhythm and
Tempo.
Words can crash like cymbals
Sing like strings
Bellow like bassoons
Flow like flautists' dreams
They can tinkle softly like triangles
Or be ponderously percussive
The human voice performs
With the instrumental range
Of a full orchestra
Either aloud
Or in your head
When a poem is read.

Villanelle

This week's poem is a villanelle
A rustic peasant form from Italy
It's difficult to pull off really well.

I can't get started, this is really hell
I'm stumped for subject matter, seriously
This week's poem is a villanelle

I wonder if my colleagues all can tell
How to write these verses brilliantly
It's difficult to pull off really well

A complicated word I couldn't spell
Its structure's left me flummoxed, as you see,
This week's poem is a villanelle

This tussle with the form sounds a death knell
For all my future lines of poetry
It's difficult to pull off really well

However much I shout and scream and yell
Assignments will not change so easily
This week's poem is a villanelle
It's difficult to pull off really well.

Midnight Dancers

A trio of ballerinas
Whirl in white
Arms aloft in arabesque
Legs leaping, feet floating
Tutus, tinged with lilac
Shimmer as they swirl
Creating a centrifuge of celestial light.
Streaks of lavender
Swish outwards from the centre
Exuberantly deepening into mauve
Until they reach the frame.

Why midnight?
Are they dancing sprites
Venturing out to play
At the witching hour
Before banishment by dawn?
These dramatic, purple shades
Suggest a depth, a profundity
'Here's a story' the artist seems to say,
'Look – herein lies mystery.'

Solar Eclipse

A humble being, a friend of Nature, ascended into heaven
Borne by wings greater and whiter than a swan
In a cloudless sky the sun hid its face in sorrow
The noonday light faded, growing pale and cold
Birds fell silent, the robin at the window stilled his song.
'Courage, humility, wisdom and kindness
Are the watchwords of a great soul'
Whispered the breeze as it softly died away.

Little by little the shadow passed over
And the sun shone again in all its majestic glory
And the daylight grew stronger and warmer
And the birds started to call to each other
And the trees waved gently in the freshening breeze
And the robin at the window sang again.

Time Tellers

Their faces tell the truth about the time
Reminding us we have so little left
We can no longer simply say 'It's fine'
While days of precious seconds are bereft.
They tick and tock relentlessly around
On wrists, on walls, on buildings, on a screen
Bejewelled glitzy watches make no sound
Their hands edge round a dial that's never seen
They do not cease, nor slow, nor give respite
To put the world on hold for just a while
Nor quicken, to precipitate the night
When morning has arisen with a smile
To conquer time there is but one defence –
Live every day with joy 'til taken hence.

Living with Joy

We often lay beneath a cherry tree
Reposing with entwinèd arms a while
Restored by warmth of touch and gentle kiss
Or gazing deep into each other's eyes
These memories were beacons in long nights
Devoid of sleep, attending to our babes.
We kept our love aflame by secret trysts
Snatched between demands of toddler years
Oases of bliss amidst the teenage strife

Years on, you lie beneath an apple tree
Within a churchyard not too far from here
While I now sit and watch our grandsons play
And wish for them the blessings we once knew
A happy, healthy fun filled life of joy
A family which builds a history
Fond memories of love that never ends
Sometimes you come to sit with me a while
And I can feel you hug me, and I smile.

About the Author

Claire-Louise Price is a writer, editor and PR consultant. She works freelance for charities and businesses and also runs creative writing workshops.

Living with Joy is her third collection of poems, forming a trilogy with *Walking with Angels*, published in 2015, and *Dancing with Love*, published in 2019.

Claire-Louise has three sons and four grandchildren and a little white dog called Polly.

Follow Claire-Louise on Facebook and Twitter @PoetryCLP

Acknowledgments

To my friends and family, too numerous to mention,
my heartfelt thanks for your support.
You know who you are.

Special thanks to my son Rob and my niece Katie
for your unwavering help and encouragement in
bringing this book to life.

The colour images are by contemporary artist
Paola Minekov, who has kindly given her permission
to reproduce her stunning paintings in this book
www.paola.art